Close to Croydon

A play

Gillian Plowman

Samuel French—London
New York-Toronto-Hollywood

FOR AMATEUR PRODUCTION ENQUIRIES

UNITED KINGDOM
plays@samuelfrench.co.uk
020 7255 4302/01

Each title is subject to availability from Samuel French, depending upon country of performance.

CLOSE TO CROYDON

First performed by the The Flat Four Players with the following cast:

Hugo Morgan	David Flint
Martha Morgan	Gillian Plowman
George Townsend	Robert Iles
Anthea	Frances Iles

CHARACTERS

Hugo Morgan; a PR consultant
Martha Morgan; Museum Education Officer
George Townsend; voice only
Anthea; voice only

The action of the play takes place in the interior of an overturned railway carriage

Time — the present

*Other plays by Gillian Plowman
published by Samuel French Ltd:*

Beata Beatrix
Cecily
David's Birthday
The Janna Years
A Kind of Vesuvius
Me and My Friend
Tippers
Two Summers
Umjana Land

CLOSE TO CROYDON

The interior of an overturned railway carriage

The play opens in darkness; a disjointed world. The Lights come up slightly. Silence. The Lights come up more, to reveal Martha and Hugo trapped in the railway carriage. They are both sitting on the floor (the ceiling of the train, originally) and are bruised and dishevelled. Martha's case is hidden in the debris

Hugo starts to sing "Rave On", the Buddy Holly song, in its Steeleye Span version

Martha (*angrily*) Do you always sing in a crisis?
Hugo I don't know. I've never been in a crisis before.
Martha Well, you're lucky then.
Hugo Done this lots of times, have you?
Martha Don't be stupid. (*She rubs one shoulder and flexes it*)
Hugo Still all right?
Martha Yes. You?
Hugo Brilliant. Considering.
Martha We're quite close to Croydon.
Hugo Close. Yes. Almost there. Probably.
Martha Almost but not quite.
Hugo Story of my life.
Martha Really?
Hugo My love life.
Martha Really.
Hugo Do you want to hear about my love life?
Martha Not really. All right. No.
Hugo That's it. You've summed up my love life.

Martha What?

Hugo I ask a beautiful woman — I love beautiful women — out for dinner — very conventional, yes I know — or to the theatre. And that's it.
"Are you free … ? Would you like to … ?"
"Not really."
Make 'em laugh. (*He sings*) "Make 'em laugh, make 'em laugh …"
"All right."
"Really?"
"No."
And there you have it. Not really. All right. No.

Pause

They say you can laugh a woman into bed.

Martha laughs very briefly

Martha That wasn't a laugh.
Hugo It wasn't much of one.
Martha Not one at all.
Hugo Still …
Martha You can't laugh a man into bed.
Hugo You've tried?
Martha No. I can't be funny. I've got no sense of humour.
Hugo Of course you have. It's the circumstances.
Martha No. I haven't. So please stop trying to amuse me.

Pause

Hugo Don't you find anything funny?
Martha Sometimes I think there's nothing funnier than a man with no clothes on, but you can't laugh, can you? You have to be beautiful. You said.
Hugo What was the last thing you laughed at?
Martha A man with no clothes on.

Hugo (*defensively*) What's funny about that?
Martha See. See.
Hugo Joke. You've got no sense of humour.
Martha My watch has stopped.

Hugo laughs. Martha looks at him in amazement

Hugo It's the way you tell 'em.
Martha It wasn't a joke.
Hugo Drunk makes a phone call. "Hallo. Is that Alcoholics Anonymous?" "Yes. Do you want to join?" "No, I want to resign."

Pause

Martha What time is it?
Hugo Eleven forty-three.
Martha Mine stopped at five past eleven.
Hugo Does it need winding up?
Martha It's broken. It obviously broke when …
Hugo Joke.
Martha That's over half an hour. How can you joke about it? Songs. Jokes. You'll break into a tap dance next.
Hugo Thirty-eight minutes.

Pause

Martha Thirty-nine!
Hugo Thirty-nine minutes. Groucho Marx taking Harpo's pulse. "Either he is dead or my watch has stopped."
Martha Shut up!

Pause

Somebody probably is dead. Have you thought of that?
Hugo They'll come soon.
Martha How do you know? (*She shivers*)

Hugo Are you cold?
Martha The heating's gone off.
Hugo Perhaps it's just as well.
Martha Why?
Hugo We could have gone up in flames.
Martha Oh for goodness' sake.
Hugo Have you got anything else to wear? In your case?
Martha How do you know I've got a case?
Hugo I sat opposite you for an hour. Remember? When we were
     the right way up? Dark blue leather case. Must have a jumper in.
Martha No. It's full of money. I've just robbed a bank.
Hugo And this is your getaway train?
Martha Yes.
Hugo Bad choice. Didn't get far. Where is it? Your case?

They search for the case. Hugo limps

Martha (*finding the case*) There it is. What's happened to your leg?
Hugo Old Irish fellow goes to the doctor. "Doctor, doctor, I've got
     a tirrible pain in me right leg." "I'm afraid it's age, Mickey," the
     doctor told him. "Now, that can't be true, doctor, for me left leg's
     exactly the same age and it's perfectly all right."
Martha Stop it!
Hugo It's not easy for me either you know — being here. I'm
     reacting. I can't help it. I'm doing it my way.
Martha (*quickly*) Don't sing.
Hugo No.
Martha I suppose you wouldn't be walking on it if it was broken.
Hugo Bruised, I expect. Now (*he repeats the Irish accent*) if we
     cover you all over with banknotes, you'll be as warm as toast. And
     wantin' for nothin'.
Martha Liberty bodices.
Hugo What?
Martha In the case.
Hugo What are they? They sound exciting …
Martha Things you wore in the war to keep you warm between
     your vest and your dress, with rubber buttons on.

Hugo Why liberty?

Martha I don't know. Ask your mother.

Hugo Perhaps because if you lasted out the war without freezing to death, there'd be liberty at the end of it.

Martha They were first made at the beginning of the twentieth century without whalebones in them. So they were flexible and comfy to wear. Gave you more liberty.

Hugo And you've got some in your case?

Martha In between the banknotes.

Hugo (*getting the case*) There you are.

Martha I'm taking them to an exhibition.

Hugo The banknotes?

Martha The liberty bodices. Educational. You know. I've got grey trousers as well. Short ones. Rites of passage going from short trousers to long trousers. Fair isle pullovers, smocked dresses. Today's kids can wear them and know what yesterday's kids … I'll never get there. We can't get out. Get out at all. Do you suffer from claustrophobia? I don't. Do you? I don't. Phew, it's hot.

Hugo It's cold.

Martha Oh yes.

Hugo So you're a teacher?

Martha Museum education. History. Past stuff. You know. What do you suffer from? Apart from a broken leg? (*She sniffs*)

Hugo Bruised. Open your case.

Martha Halitosis?

Hugo You tell me. (*He leans towards her and breathes out*)

Martha No. God, it's something else. Gas. Do you think there's gas leaking, or chemicals or something.

Hugo It's an electric train.

Martha Electricity. Does electricity leak?

Hugo No.

Martha What do you think it is then? The train's upside down!

Hugo I don't know. Scorching.

Martha Scorching?

Hugo Brakes. Oil. I don't know. You thought it was my breath? Thank you very much.

Martha No. I didn't. Scorching? Brakes? Oil?

Hugo Show me the liberty bodices.
Martha I can't get my case open.
Hugo Here …
Martha It's locked.
Hugo It would be, with all that money inside. Did you do it on your own?
Martha What?
Hugo Rob the bank?
Martha Yes. Women can, you know.
Hugo It's not the women bit I'm amazed at, it's the on your own bit. No accomplices?
Martha No. It only leads to arguments. (*She shivers*)

Hugo takes his jacket off and puts it round Martha's shoulders

Hugo Here. Have my jacket.
Martha I don't know where my key is.
Hugo Where did you put it?
Martha In my bag. I don't know where my bag is.
Hugo It'll be here somewhere.

They search for Martha's handbag

Martha It's not. It's gone. How? How? How can it have got out and gone? And we can't. We can't.
Hugo You're not going to cry, are you?
Martha How long is it now?
Hugo Fifty-one minutes.
Martha No. I might do when it's sixty minutes. Oh God. Oh God. I don't know what to do. We can't help anybody, can we? Do you think people are dead? And … and … the driver. Do you think he's dead? (*She sinks to the ground*)
Hugo (*sitting beside Martha and putting his arm round her*) There's no reason to believe that anybody's dead.
Martha I don't panic normally.
Hugo You do it on a skidpan with a bunch of bananas on your head.
Martha No, I don't.

Hugo No. Of course you don't.

Pause

Little Tommy was eight and the apple of his strictly Methodist parents' eyes — a good little boy who never put a foot wrong until the day he didn't want to eat his sprouts.

Martha Bananas. Sprouts.

Hugo Are you hungry?

Martha No.

Hugo "They're good for you, Tommy, eat them up."
  "No."
  "But they're good for you."
  "No."
  "Don't disobey Mummy."
  "I don't want them."
  "God says you must honour and obey your father and your mother, He'll be very cross."
  To no avail.
  "The sprouts are going back in the fridge till you come to your senses."
  Later that evening, a storm sprang up. Thunder. Lightning. More lightning. Claps of thunder. Bursts of thunder. Gale force winds. Crashing hail storms. The father and mother heard Tommy's bedroom door open; his footsteps coming down the stairs, going into the kitchen; the fridge door opening. They peeked in. Sure enough, Tommy was eating the offending vegetables. And his clear little voice muttered, "Helluva fuss to make, God, about a few bloody sprouts."

There is a muffled banging. They leap to their feet

The voice of George Townsend can be heard

George (*off*) Hallo. Hallo. Can you hear me?
Hugo } (*together*) Yes.
Martha }

George (*off*) Is anybody there?
Hugo   ⎱
Martha   ⎰ (*together*) Yes, yes.
Martha Oh, thank God.
Hugo Can you get us out?
George (*off*) Is anybody there?

The voice gets clearer

   Is anybody there?
Hugo   ⎱
Martha   ⎰ (*together, shouting*) Yes!
George (*off*) Will one person speak please.
Martha You.
Hugo (*to George*) Yes.
George (*off*) How many of you are there?
Hugo Two.
George (*off*) Only two in the carriage?
Hugo Yes.
George (*off*) Are you injured?
Hugo No.
Martha (*to Hugo*) Yes, you are.
Hugo (*to Martha*) Not in the scheme of things.
George (*off*) Neither of you?
Hugo There's a lady … you have to get her out. We're trapped in
   here.
George (*off*) What are her injuries?
Martha (*to George*) Please, please get us out.
George (*off*) We will. I promise. We'll have to cut you out. The
   equipment is on its way. There's nothing to worry about. Try to
   relax. Breathe deeply and relax. My name is George. George
   Townsend. Will you tell me your names, please.
Hugo Hugo Morgan.

Martha looks at Hugo. He looks enquiringly at her

Martha (*to Hugo*) Martha Morgan.

Hugo (*to Martha*) Really?

She nods

    And Martha Morgan.
George (*off*) Married?

Hugo looks at Martha enquiringly

Martha Divorced.
Hugo We're divorced.
George (*off*) Never mind. I'm sure you're still very fond of each
    other.
Martha No …
Hugo (*to Martha*) It doesn't matter … (*To George*) How long will
    it take, do you think?

No reply

    George? George!

No reply

Martha He's gone.
Hugo To get on with things. I'm sure ——
Martha (*shouting over*) George! George! Is anybody dead? Is the
    driver dead? (*To Hugo*) Why has he gone away?
Hugo He's gone to check out the rest of the train.
Martha If it's a disaster ——
Hugo It's not a disaster. We're fine, aren't we? Funny about ——
Martha If it's a disaster, I mean people will know about it … it'll
    be on the news, that the train's crashed, and people have died and
    my mother will … she's got a weak heart, you see … she knows
    I'm on this train … she's interested in my work … she found the
    liberty bodices for me originally … an elderly friend of hers … in
    the war, she'd taken her children to a friend's house and left them
    there wrapped in blankets because she wanted to wash all their

clothes ready for them to be evacuated to the country. And a bomb dropped on the friend's house and the children were killed and all she had left were their clothes which she kept all these years until she gave them to my mother for me. And now my mother ——

Hugo I imagined myself making love to you, you know.

Martha What?

Hugo In that hour before.

Martha What?

Hugo You were looking out of the window, dreaming. I wondered what about. I liked your legs. It got warm. You took your coat off and stood up to put it on the rack on top of your case and you stretched up and I wanted to put my hands around your waist. You're very beautiful.

Martha For goodness' sake ——

Hugo When the others got off, and we were alone, what did you think?

Martha Nothing.

Hugo You weren't frightened?

Martha No.

Hugo Being alone with a strange man?

Martha It was broad daylight.

Hugo Didn't you feel me staring at you?

Pause

Martha I was going to move, actually. Get my coat down, get my case down. But it's heavy, so you'd probably have helped me and then either we'd both be standing together and you'd know why I was going and that would have been a direct accusation — I mean it would have seemed rude. I'd have felt embarrassed.

Hugo Or?

Martha Or ... um ...

Hugo No, you should have gone. I was going to kiss you.

Martha What?

Hugo That's what I was thinking. I'd like to kiss you and make love to you.

Martha What then? There? Here?

Hugo That's what I was thinking when I was looking at you.
Martha And you were going to do it?
Hugo That's what I was thinking …
Martha You're talking about rape. You were going to rape me? What the hell are you talking about? You're saying that —
Hugo Why didn't you go? It was a risk.
Martha I don't know. Because I don't believe that every man you're left alone with is a potential rapist. What are you saying? How can you say that? I don't believe that … I know what you're … you're saying that I could have been in a worse situation if the train hadn't crashed?
Hugo Yes.
Martha Could I? Could I?
Hugo Yes.
Martha Well, if you'd told me this before, I could have been having a really nice time for the last hour! I just didn't know how lucky I was!
Hugo That's what I'm saying.
Martha A rave. I'd have been having a rave.
Hugo I'm saying it could have been worse.
Martha What do you do for a living?
Hugo I'm in PR. Public relations.
Martha (*bursting out laughing*) Employed by Railtrack to make train crashes look good.
Hugo I've made you laugh.
Martha You haven't made me laugh. That was scornful derision and disbelief.
Hugo No, I am in PR.
Martha Well, you're no bloody good at it. Public relations. How do you think I feel now? Would you have raped me or was it all in the mind? Are you going to rape me now? Is it still in your mind? I am trapped with you in a … no chance of getting my case down and moving to the next compartment. I can't get away. How the hell do you think I feel now?
Hugo I'm sorry. I —— (*He steps towards her*)
Martha No. Stay where you are. I don't believe it. I don't believe for a minute that you would have done it. But *why* did you say it?

Hugo Because I'm fed up with you. Carrying on. Panicking. Wingeing. Why am I supposed to be manly and brave, calming you down and cheering you up and sorting out your luggage and keeping you warm? Don't you think my mother's going to be worried about me? Don't you think I'm worried about my mother being worried about me? And I've got a major client who will be pacing the floor and giving my contract to someone else, despite whatever excuse I come up with ...

Martha Being in a train crash ...

Hugo Won't cut any ice with him. Last week my wife was awarded custody of my kids, on Sunday I was burgled and yesterday someone jostled me and I dropped my mobile phone off Waterloo Bridge. Otherwise I would have been prepared for today. Wouldn't I? Wouldn't I?

Pause

Martha Right.

Hugo I was just thinking, that's all, just thinking. You can't go to gaol for what you're thinking.

Martha Don't sing!

Hugo That's how it starts. Don't let anyone tell you otherwise. You look at a woman and imagine making love to her. No-one ever knows about your thought. You even dismiss it from your own mind. If the woman is just a stranger on a train, you'll never even speak to her. See her again. If she's a business contact, you get on with business. But if you ever want to get to know a woman better, it's because that bit has come first.

Martha Right.

Hugo That bit comes first. I'm sorry. I know it's politically incorrect but at least I'm honest. I fancied you.

Martha Past tense? You've got over it?

Hugo Have you seen yourself lately? Anyway, you get over it. Other things infiltrate?

Martha Like what?

Hugo A woman's voice. As soon as she speaks ... my libido is invariably punctured by a high little voice.

Martha (*in a voice that comes out too high*) I don't … (*She coughs and makes her voice low*) I don't know …

Pause

Hugo You've got to trust your instincts.

She nearly laughs

Watch it. You nearly laughed. What?
Martha Nothing.
Hugo Tell me.
Martha No.

There is muffled banging, then the voice of Anthea

Anthea (*off*) Mr and Mrs Morgan?
Hugo Yes!
Anthea (*off*) Can you hear me?
Hugo Yes!
Anthea (*off*) Can you hear me?
Martha How can we hear them but not them us?
Hugo They've got loudspeakers or microphones or something. (*He shouts*) Yes!
Anthea (*off*) Mr and Mrs Morgan?
Hugo Shout together.
Hugo ⎱ (*together, shouting*) Yes!
Martha ⎰
Anthea (*off*) My name is Anthea. I'm your contact.
Hugo What happened to George?
Anthea (*off*) Can you hear me? Mr and Mrs Morgan?
Hugo ⎱ (*together, shouting*) Yes!
Martha ⎰
Anthea Help is on its way. The cutting equipment is coming. Please relax. Are you injured?

Hugo doesn't reply. Martha looks at him

Martha Hugo?
Hugo I can't shout.
Martha Why not? Hugo?
Anthea (*off*) Mr Morgan? Mrs Morgan?
Hugo Lost me breath.
Anthea (*off*) Hugo? Martha?
Martha (*to Anthea*) Has my mother rung?
Anthea (*off*) I'm sorry. Speak up.
Martha (*shouting*) Has my mother rung?
Anthea (*off*) I can't hear you.
Hugo (*shouting*) Has Martha's mother rung? She'll be very
   worried …

Hugo coughs into his handkerchief, sounding very ill

Martha (*shouting*) And so will Hugo's.

He coughs

   Oh, my God. Oh my God Hugo. You're bleeding. (*She shouts*)
   Anthea. Hugo is hurt. Anthea?
Anthea (*off*) I heard you.
Martha He's coughing up blood.
Hugo I'm coughing up blood.
Martha You'd better sit down.
Anthea (*off*) Sit your husband down. Martha? Mrs Morgan?
Hugo I … I … don't feel … I'm not in pain or anything. Just a clot
   or something.
Martha A clot?
Hugo A clot?
Martha Oh God, a clot.
Anthea (*off*) Mrs Morgan?
Martha He's got a clot or something. (*To Hugo*) Sit down.
Anthea (*off*) Slightly reclining if you can. And keep him warm. It
   won't be long now.
Martha (*to Hugo*) Sit!
Hugo I love a dominant woman.

Martha And have your jacket back.
Hugo Now you'll get cold.
Martha Relax. (*Shouts*) Anthea!
Hugo You relax. She's got a high voice.
Martha Anthea?
Hugo Anthea.

Pause

My wife had the most beautiful voice.
Martha Did she?
Hugo So many people fell in love with her voice. In the end she fell
in love with one back. And left me.

Pause

Martha This wonderful old lady in the East End — Dolly — that
I went to see whilst collecting clothes from the war told me her
husband came home on two days leave, bringing a friend with
him, and they all had to sleep in the air-raid shelter. But her
husband, Reggie, loved his breakfast and always knew where to
lay his hands on a chop or a couple of sausages, 'cos he had
contacts. So in the morning he went off to find some breakfast,
learning on the way that an unexploded bomb had landed in the
back yard of the house next door. However, determined to have
his breakfast, he didn't tell Dolly or his friend and they all went
into the house for a big fry-up. And all the time he was walking
round like this: (*she gets up and walks about, very loose-limbed
and floppy*) Dolly thought he looked odd, but he said, "Go on, you
try it," and they were all walking around like this (*she walks about
again, all floppy*) ... giggling away. And they had a wonderful
breakfast. And Reggie said, "Right, follow me ..." and they all
walked out of the house. (*She walks about again, all floppy*) By
which time, Dolly wanted to know what it was all about, so
Reggie told her about the unexploded bomb, but said that as long
as they were all relaxed when the bomb went off, they wouldn't
sustain any injuries.

Hugo (*smiling*) You're developing a sense of humour.
Martha It's being married to you.
Hugo Yes, that's funny, isn't it? Having the same name?
Martha Hilarious.
Hugo A rave.

There is a long silence

What about in a posing pouch?
Martha What?
Hugo If you don't like men with no clothes on, what about in a posing pouch?
Martha Being in PR, you'd wear an imposing pouch.
Hugo Not being sure of anything, you'd wear a supposing pouch.
Martha Dustman — disposing pouch.
Hugo Tony Blair — opposing pouch.
Martha Man on bended knee — proposing pouch.
Hugo Investigative journalist — exposing pouch.
Martha Graphic designer — superimposing pouch.
Hugo Military junta — deposing pouch.
Martha Musician — composing pouch.
Hugo Dead body — decomposing pouch.
Martha Oh God …

Pause

Hugo You don't like singing, do you?
Martha Yes, I do.
Hugo You've changed.
Martha It's being married to you.
Hugo Shall we sing?
Martha Aren't you out of breath?
Hugo Recovered.
Martha OK. What?
Hugo (*singing*) Oh God our help in ages past
Hugo
Martha } (*in unison*) Our hope for years to come

> Our shelter from the stormy blast
> And our eternal home.

Pause

Hugo sings the verse from "Rave On" he sang earlier, snapping his fingers. Martha joins in and they sing in harmony

Hugo You know that?
Martha Steeleye Span.
Hugo You're my ideal woman. (*He starts to cough*)
Martha Don't cough. Don't cough. Don't cough. (*She wraps her arms around Hugo as though to stop the cough*) What do you think's the matter with you?
Hugo My image. It's really not very impressive at the moment.
Martha I shouldn't worry about that.

Martha sits Hugo down and remains with him, hugging him

Hugo I have to worry about image. That's my job. People and organizations need to take care how they present themselves to the world.
Martha Even if it's not the truth?
Hugo I don't work for anyone or anything I don't believe in.
Martha You're called in, are you, to different organizations? To work on their image?
Hugo Yes.
Martha Lots of different organizations?
Hugo Yes.
Martha You can't believe in them all.
Hugo Yes, I do.
Martha But you don't change anything.
Hugo Their image.
Martha Polluting industries made to look green, but still polluting. Changing their image doesn't change anything. Aren't you just concerned with what *seems* to be rather than what is?
Hugo No.

Martha I don't understand. If you are making something, or
providing a service, it has to be good and you have to do it well
and honestly, and you have to care about what you do, and it's up
to you to make your own image, which should be called reputa-
tion, not to Hugo Morgan who is nothing to do with you.

Hugo I'm a professional and I can do it better. And that will help
you to succeed in whatever you care about, expand even, employ
more people.

Martha Bigger isn't always better. Look at supermarkets.

Hugo Generally agreed to be a good thing.

Martha Not by corner shops, little old ladies and people without
cars. And people without cars don't pollute.

Hugo I'm as green as the next man.

Martha (*looking at Hugo*) You are (*she feels his forehead*) green.
And wet.

Hugo You make me sound like a jungle.

*Martha looks for something to wipe his forehead with. She can't get
into her case and kicks it*

Martha Shit! Shit! Bloody case. (*She wipes his head with her hands
and wipes them on her clothes*) You're dripping.

Hugo Thank you.

Martha Why? Why are you sweating? It's cold.

Hugo It's very cold.

Martha takes her coat off and puts it round Hugo

What do I look like?

Martha What about the person inside you? Who's there? You're
so busy with image. Anthea should be back soon.

Hugo The go-between — an interposing pouch.

Martha Two people at odds with one another — a juxtaposing
pouch.

Hugo Who's that? You and me?

Martha No.

Hugo Why are you divorced?

Martha Grew apart, that's all.
Hugo So who is there in your life?
Martha Just at the moment, there's you.
Hugo We were destined to meet.
Martha That's bollocks.
Hugo So who is there?
Martha You know what I was thinking? In that hour before?
Hugo What?
Martha I was actually wondering what sort of a sperm count you had?
Hugo What? My sperm count?
Martha My husband had a low sperm count, you see, and I never got pregnant.
Hugo You want to get pregnant?
Martha I was only thinking. My age. And single now. I don't stand a chance of any fertility treatment and I'd have to pay the earth for artificial insemination. Even then, would I know what I was getting. That's why I was wondering about your sperm count.
Hugo Never had it measured.
Martha No.
Hugo How were you going to get it?
Martha Well, I suppose I was I going to try and … I wasn't going to do anything. I was just thinking about it, that's all.
Hugo You were going to try and rape me.
Martha You can't rape men. Women can't.
Hugo You were after my sperm! That's rape.
Martha No it's not!
Hugo Yes, it is. Nothing to do with me. With caring about me. There you were, being all superior about image, and what about the person inside, and all the time you wanted my sperm because I appear, I repeat *appear*, to be a good-looking, intelligent male of the species.
Martha Have you seen yourself lately?
Hugo (*in pain; sadly*) No. Don't look at me then. (*He begins to retch and shiver*)
Martha (*enfolding Hugo*) No, no. You're beautiful. Lovely. We'll soon dry you out. Have you ever been dried out before? Big log

fire. Would you like to dry out in front of that. In a comfy arm
chair?
Hugo Yes.

There is a pause

(*Closing his eyes*) Someone who's going to sleep ...
Martha Reposing pouch?
Hugo Martha, would you have dinner with me?
Martha Yes. Yes, I'd love to.
Hugo Would you ——
Martha Yes.
Hugo Not today.
Martha We're a bit tied up today.
Hugo Another day. And ...
Martha What?

Hugo lapses into unconsciousness

Hugo. What?
Hugo (*coming round momentarily*) Would you go and see my
mother?
Martha Yes.
Hugo And ...
Martha You're a very demanding person.

The Lights dim

Oh, no ...

And come up again

Oh God. Let there be light. Hugo. Hugo. I've got a joke. Listen.
It's about when God was a woman, and she'd made the earth and
everything and then she said "Let there be light" and there was
light. And then she said, "I don't know. Can I see the dark again,
please?"

Hugo is dead. There is a long silence

Hugo …

She sings the verse from "Rave On" again

CURTAIN

FURNITURE AND PROPERTY LIST

Further dressing may be added at the director's discretion

On stage: **Martha**'s case

LIGHTING PLOT

Practical fittings required: nil

To open: Darkness

Cue 1   When ready   (Page 1)
Bring up light slowly; pause; bring them up more

Cue 2   **Martha**: "You're a very demanding person."   (Page 20)
Dim lights

Cue 3   **Martha**: "Oh, no ... "   (Page 20)
Bring lights up full again

www.ingramcontent.com/pod-product-compliance
Ingram Content Group UK Ltd.
Pitfield, Milton Keynes, MK11 3LW, UK
UKHW021817150726
7214IPUK00017B/173